THE BAT
GUIT
FOOTBA

Written by Sam Kotadia

Psychologist Sam Kotadia professionally helps top flight footballers stay focused and conquer the Bad Loser that lurks within us all. With this series of playful guides, Sam chucks his expertise out the window and offers strategies that are sure to lead to failure at every turn.

Illustrated by Nick Hilditch

Illustrator Nick Hilditch went off golf as a child when his Dad made him caddy for him in exchange for pocket money. So, in a way, his Bad Loser got the better of him before he'd ever taken a swing. His sport of choice is piercing inflated egos with the pointiest of pointy pencils. He teamed up with Sam to bring his skewed vision and irreverence to the Bad Loser's highly questionable advice.

Enjoy the game!

TO

....

FROM

....

Don't blame
the referee

Decisions that go against you during the game are clearly the referee's fault!

You haven't been perfecting the art of football since you were 3 years old for nothing.

It is your responsibility to correct the referee when they get it wrong with abuse and treating them with utter contempt. It will help them in the long-run.

Don't get distracted by the crowd

There is no harm in show-boating in front of the crowd.

They have paid good money to come and see you.

Outrageous goal celebrations, heckling the opposition fan base, and keeping your eye out for that Real Madrid scout is clearly acceptable.

Make sure that you warm up properly

Warm-ups? Are you having a laugh?

You were born ready!

Warming up is for wimps.

You don't get injuries when you are made of steel, so clearly there is no need.

Celebrate tastefully

If you decide to score a goal, make sure that the whole world knows about it. As well as pulling off your most spectacular celebration, make sure everyone on that pitch knows how great you are.

Most importantly get
it on camera!
This will help you to
remind friends and family
what a gift you are to the
game. Evening entertainment
for the whole family; who
needs the cinema?

Don't blame
your team-mates

The only downside to football is that you have to rely on 10 other players to pull their weight. Although your skills alone are usually enough to win most matches, it is still frustrating when you are the only one with any talent.

To make it clear to your teammates what you expect of them, expose their mistakes and weaknesses in front of the crowd, and the opposition. Tough love is the best medicine.

Stay off the booze at half-time

Fortunately for someone with your talents, a couple bottles of light spirits at half-time makes no difference to your footballing prowess.

If anything, coming out at half-time slightly drunk adds to the occasion. It makes the game a little more challenging for you, and ensures that all 50/50 tackles are met with full force!

Go in hard at all times!

Congratulate your opponents if they win

In the unlikely event that your opponents win the match remind them that anyone can win the lottery!

Whilst shaking hands is considered the sporting way to end the competition, make it your sole purpose to remind them that luck was the only factor in securing their victory. Your useless teammates also helped them!

Respect the linesmen
at all times

Linesmen are a sad breed of humans. Failed footballers who have finally realised that they are talentless and now find comfort in making the lives of others a misery...

You cannot avoid the constant barrage of poor decisions linesmen make, so save your aggression and anger for more worthy causes. Don't even acknowledge them!

Make sure
that you tackle fairly

All tackles are fair in your eyes.

Tackling is all about the survival of the fittest.

If you break a leg, run it off!

There is no such thing as an injury, it is all in the mind!

No handballs

It only becomes a handball if you get caught!

If your cunning fools the referee and the linesmen, then you are entitled to the rewards.

However, the only time you start using your hands during a game of football is when you are bored.

It adds a new dimension to the game, and most importantly, it irritates the opposition.

The Bad Losers Guides ™

Published by Mindsport Ltd in 2012- All rights reserved. Printed in China

Illustration copyright © Nick Hilditch